Kerri –
With love!
Robin Jones Gunn
x
Rachel Gunn

Gentle Passages

Guiding Your Daughter | Robin
| Jones
into Womanhood | Gunn

Multnomah Gifts®

Multnomah® Publishers *Sisters, Oregon*

When Hearts Are Young

Come to me when my heart is young

Let tender words roll off your tongue

Reveal the sweet mysteries one by one

when my heart is young

Come to me when my ears are small

Before my thoughts have heard it all

Whisper clearly God's gentle call

when my ears are small

Come to me when my eyes are clear

Before my heart has learned to fear

Show me the beauty in all you hold dear

when my eyes are clear

Come to me when my frame is straight

Before my peers don't hesitate

Promise me the blessing for those who wait

when my frame is straight

Come to me and be the one

Who guides me till this journey's done

And on the other shore I've become

A woman like you

with a heart still young

As the Journey Begins

*When it comes to womanhood,
all women are sisters,
and all sisters share secrets.*

Welcome to a collection of secrets meant to be shared between sisters.

Perhaps you picked up this book because you know a special young girl who is about to embark on the journey into womanhood. Her heart is young, her eyes are clear, and she is looking to you for guidance.

Yet you hesitate. How can you whisper the truths of womanhood to her when the memory of your own passage is not necessarily pleasant? Perhaps, like me, you had sufficient information but certainly no celebration. No tradition to look forward to carrying on to the next generation.

When a young woman's body is about to change, she leans in for instruction. Often such advice is offered with serious expressions and foreboding murmurs about PMS. Where is the joy in this miraculous journey into womanhood?

Like many mothers, I wanted to give my daughter more than I had. But how? What? I saw myself as the reluctant guide ferrying a small craft across misty waters. I knew the way from the island of childhood innocence to the mainland of womanhood simply because I had made the crossing myself. I never considered going back and charting a calm and lovely course for anyone else.

Yet it happened. Naturally. Wonderfully. And each segment of the journey was a celebration. An establishing of new traditions.

I made several crossings, not only with my daughter but also with other girls who trusted me to steer them across the unfamiliar waters. The journeys were amazing. They were God-moments—those times when something eternal happens, and you simply watch God work.

I told a few friends about these journeys. My friends listened with their eyes glistening and their imaginations filling with plans to gently guide a certain young heart across the waters. Each of my friends said the same thing, "I want to do what you did. Would you write it all down for me?" I promised I would. This book is the keeping of that promise.

I pray that from these pages you will hear whispers of encouragement. And that you will joyfully, freely come alongside a young heart and make her journey into womanhood a gentle passage.

We have a young sister…. What shall we do

for our sister for the day she is spoken for?

SONG OF SONGS 8:8

THE SECRET OF

THE FINE CHINA PLATE

*Y*ears ago on a blissful summer afternoon, I settled into the backyard hammock. My children were napping in their rooms. Beside me sat a basket filled with ripe apricots and plump, dark cherries. Overhead the white clouds floated lazily across the turquoise sky like a gathering of elegant swans.

That's when my friend, nine-year-old Natalie, came over and flopped onto a lawn chair with a heavy sigh.

"Are you hungry?" I asked. "Would you like an apricot?"

She shook her head.

"Is everything okay?"

She shrugged.

"Come on." I slipped out of the hammock. "Let's go inside and wash this fruit."

She shuffled into the kitchen behind me. I ran the water over the soft apricots and waited for her to speak.

"All my friends went to the movies without me," Natalie said at last. "My parents said it wasn't the kind of movie I should see."

"Oh?"

"Yeah, my parents are too protective. They said they wanted me to stay clean. What is that supposed to mean?"

I gently shook the glistening fruit and placed it in a bowl. Earlier that day I had prepared a pan of melted chocolate so my toddlers could dip the cherries when they woke up. I decided to warm the chocolate and give it a trial run.

"My parents don't understand how awful it is to be the only one left out. They don't remember what it's like to be a kid. It's different now than it was when they were my age. It's just not fair."

I dipped the first few cherries, and they came out looking delicious.

"What are you going to do with those cherries?" Natalie asked.

"I thought I'd serve them to my guest. Would you like them?"

Natalie nodded. Her expression had turned hopeful.

"Let me put them on a plate for you." I rummaged through the kitchen garbage and pulled out a paper plate stained with beans and hot dogs from last night's barbecue.

"You're not going to use that dirty plate, are you?"

I shrugged, holding the plate in one hand and the cherries in the other, waiting.

"Don't you have any other plates you could use?" Natalie asked.

"Oh yes." I returned the paper plate to the garbage and the cherries to the pan of warm chocolate. "I have a few other plates. They're special plates. Clean plates. Plates that I keep set apart from all the others."

Natalie watched as I unclasped the antique hutch's glass door and lifted out a single, fine china plate. "I'm probably overly protective of these plates," I told her.

"You should be protective," Natalie said. "Those are valuable plates."

"Yes, I suppose they are." I handed the plate to her. "Maybe that's why I want to keep them clean and ready so I can use them to serve others."

A flicker of understanding floated across Natalie's face. "It's beautiful." She traced the gold trim around the outside of the plate.

"Yes," I agreed. "Special gifts that have been set apart have a beauty all their own, don't they?"

Natalie tilted her head. "Why are you smiling like that?"

"I'm smiling because you're beautiful, Natalie. You're more valuable than you can ever imagine. You are a special gift from God. Don't you see? You've been set apart, just like a fine china plate."

Natalie sat down and stared at the china plate in her hands as if she were memorizing all the delicate details. "And that's why my parents wouldn't let me go to the movies, isn't it? When they said they wanted me to stay clean it's because they want me to be set apart. That's why they're so protective." Natalie's voice grew soft and small. "And china plates don't go around getting smeared with beans and hot dogs, do they?"

"Not usually."

Natalie's brown eyes narrowed as she shifted her gaze and examined me the same way she had been studying the tiny flowers on the plate. "Did my mom call you before I came over?"

"No."

"Then how did you know to tell me all this stuff? Where did you learn it?"

I paused before leaning closer and whispering, "From the Bible."

"The Bible doesn't say anything about special plates!"

"Oh, doesn't it?" I went upstairs, retrieved my Bible, and placed it on the kitchen table next to Natalie. Picking up the china plate, I returned to the kitchen where I found a permanent marker and wrote on the back of the plate. I then arranged a clump of chocolate-covered cherries on the clean plate. They settled into a little puddle of chocolate.

Intrigue danced across Natalie's face as she looked up from the opened Bible and watched me present her with the elegant treat. "Where is it?" she asked.

"Where's what?"

"The secret verse in the Bible about the china plate."

"You'll find what you're looking for on the back of this plate."

Natalie carefully looked underneath the plate and read the words I had just written with the permanent marker:

> For Natalie, You are God's fine china plate.
> Love always, Robin
> 2 Timothy 2:21

Natalie reached for the Bible. She read aloud from 2 Timothy, "'If you stay away from sin you will be like one of these dishes made of purest gold—the very best in the house—so that Christ himself can use you for his highest purposes'" (TLB).

Her eyes grew wide. "You were right! It is in the Bible!"

"And you were right about your parents being protective of you. They're helping you to make good choices by keeping you set apart and clean, just like a fine china plate. One day Christ Himself will use you for His highest purposes."

She popped one of the cherries in her mouth. "What do you think His highest purposes are?"

I pointed to the china plate. "What is the plate doing right now?"

"Shining?"

"Yes, it's shining because it's clean. The plate is also serving you. That's how God will use you as His fine china plate. He will use you to serve others."

When Natalie left my home that afternoon, she carefully balanced in her hands my little gift to her, the signed, fine china plate. Her mother hung it on her bedroom wall. Her friends asked why it was there. Over the years she told others the story again and again of how she wanted always to be set apart, just like a fine china plate.

Last year, on a blissful summer afternoon, while creamy clouds swam like elegant swans in a turquoise sky, I sat in a small church. A crowd had gathered for the joyful celebration. The music rose, and so did we. Down the aisle came a breathtakingly beautiful bride dressed in pure white. I couldn't take my eyes off Natalie's face. Promises kept, hopes fulfilled, childhood questions now answered, Natalie floated down that aisle, and her face was shining.

Just like a fine china plate.

Once in an age, God sends to us someone
who loves us…not alone with emotion,
but with understanding.
HARRIET BEECHER STOWE

Dear Robin,

I only have a few minutes, but I had to write you this note. The table is set for four. The tea is brewing. The food is ready. And I am sitting here, waiting for three very special Fine China Plates to arrive. Tonight I will give to someone else what you gave to me more than ten years ago.

I have never forgotten that day when I watched you digging through the kitchen garbage for a used paper plate. I thought you were crazy! Then you took down that china plate from the cupboard and proceeded to tell me how I was set apart and that I was a fine china plate.

In a wealthy home there are dishes made of gold and silver as well as some made from wood and clay. The expensive dishes are used for guests, and the cheap ones are used in the kitchen or to put garbage in. If you stay away from sin you will be like one of these dishes made of purest gold—the very best in the house—so that Christ himself can use you for his highest purposes. Run from anything that gives you the evil thoughts… but stay close to anything that makes you want to do right. Have faith and love, and enjoy the companionship of those who love the Lord and have pure hearts.

2 TIMOTHY 2:20–22 [TLB]

As I look back now, I realize that something happened that day. A thought began. As deeper understanding grew, it established a mind-set, which turned into a lifestyle.

Tonight I seek to invest in three young girls and to give to them the secret you gave me that summer day. I feel as if you should be here. I bought china plates for each of them and wrote on the back with a permanent marker. Hopefully Erica, Lauren, and Tessa will understand more deeply after tonight how special they are and what a privilege it is to be set apart.

One day I know God will use them for His highest purposes, which are, as you taught me, being clean and ready so He can use us to serve others.

Oh, there's the doorbell! Thank you, Robin. I cannot tell you how grateful I am.

Love always,
Natalie

Celebration Suggestions from My Friends

DIEDRA: My heritage is British-Canadian. I have three daughters. On each of my daughters' tenth birthdays, we went shopping with my mum and grandmum, and the birthday daughter chose her china pattern. Great-grandmum bought each girl her first china plate that day. Each time, we went to tea after shopping and asked the waiter to serve the honored daughter on her new china plate.

Over the years the girls were served on their special plates on a number of occasions. We filled one daughter's china plate with raw carrots and served them in the living room the night her braces were removed. Another daughter found her plate in front of her at a mother-daughter tea at church where she was to sing a duet. Our oldest daughter used her plate to hold the first slice of her wedding cake before she and her groom served each other a bite.

MARIAN: I am old enough to have grandchildren, but since I never married, I've enjoyed doting on my sister's grandchildren. When my first great-niece was nine, I sent her an invitation to a picnic for just the two of us. I found a secluded spot near the rose garden at our park and spread out an old bedspread in the shade. She was surprised when I pulled out what she called "fancy" plates to serve our meal. I told her I had eaten off these plates every day for twenty-three years while I was a missionary in China. They had been a gift to me when I first arrived in Canton.

For our picnic we drank lemonade and ate heart-shaped sandwiches and tiny lemon tarts with raspberries on top. I told my niece that she was special and set apart, just like a fine china plate. Then I told her she could keep the plate because I had written her name and an important Bible verse on the back.

Her mother later told me my great-niece wrapped the plate in a towel and slept with it for three nights before asking that it be kept in the china hutch for her.

MELISSA: When my college roommate told me about her childhood, she said she wished she could start over and have her innocence back. A few days later she and I were at a thrift store, and I found a beautiful china plate that was buried under a lot of junk. She couldn't believe I wanted to buy it and tried to convince me the price was too high.

That night I surprised her with a special tea party in our dorm room complete with candles, cake, and jasmine tea. The white china plate from the thrift store cleaned up beautifully, and I served her cake on it. I told her that in God's eyes she was just as beautiful, pure, and white as the plate she now held in her lap. I told her that God had come looking for her, and when He found her, He paid an extravagant price for her, washed her, and made her clean. Then I told her that the plate in her lap was the same discarded plate I had bought that morning at the thrift store. She burst into tears.

For the rest of our junior year, that pure white china plate sat on the dresser next to her mirror. I suggested once that we could hang it on the wall. But she said she wanted to keep it right where it was. Every time she looked in her mirror, that china plate reminded her of how God saw her.

 Items you need before passing on the secret of the fine china plate:
- A china plate of any shape, size, or color
- A permanent marker that works on china
- A plate hanger or plate stand, if the china is to be displayed
- Preparations for a special party that will accompany the presentation of the plate

Other suggested items:
- Matching china cup and saucer to be used with the plate for future celebrations
- Videos or books on women in history who were set apart and used by God

INTO WOMANHOOD

$\mathcal{I}$ watch my ten-year-old daughter paint her fingernails while I fold the laundry in the living room.

"Tana got press-on nails," Rachel tells me. "When she had to scratch her nose at lunch today, she went like this." Rachel demonstrates how Tana held her finger a half-inch from the end of her nose and opened her mouth in a perfect, tiny O.

"I see." I try not to laugh.

"I was thinking of getting press-on nails with my birthday money. Meredith said she's going to get some, too. What do you think?"

What do I think? I think a ten-year-old does not need fake nails or fake anything! All I say is, "Hmmm."

"Meredith is going to get her hair highlighted this summer. I want to highlight mine, too. Don't you think my hair would look better if it was lighter?"

"I think your hair is beautiful just the way it is."

"No it isn't! I hate my hair. It's too short, too thick, and too dark."

I look at this blossoming beauty sprawled on the couch with her bottle of nail polish carefully balanced on a paper towel. Nothing is too short, too thick, or too dark about her. I think she is adorable. No, more than adorable, she is beautiful. I think she is amazing, fresh, and gorgeous.

But I don't know how to tell her.

So I silently fold the towels and carry them upstairs.

During the next week, I listen. Rachel tells me she needs a new type of toothpaste, one that whitens teeth. She is convinced she needs to pluck her eyebrows and wash her face with peach scrub instead of soap. She receives her first invitation to a boy-girl party at the ice-skating rink. And she bursts into tears when her brother tells her it's her turn to feed the dog.

There's no denying it; all the signs are there. My little girl is skipping—no, dashing—toward womanhood. And I can't stop her or slow her down.

However, there might be something I can do....

Something more than drive her to dance lessons on Tuesdays and soccer practice on Thursdays. Something more than answer her increasing phone calls. I want to do more than buy her a magazine that combines fashion tips with advice on healthy snacks, and instruction in the fine art of eyebrow plucking. I also know that when the inevitable moment comes, I want to do more than present her with a box of pads and hide my embarrassment as I close her bedroom door on my way out, muttering, "Let me know if you have any questions."

But what can I do?

For days I think about how to make her entrance into womanhood a memorable celebration. I want it to be a special time of sharing secrets between the two of us.

All the pieces come together on a snowy Saturday night in February. The guys are gone, and Rachel and I have the house to ourselves. I start a fire in the fireplace and tell Rachel I'd like her to join me for a tea party. I'm wearing a nice outfit so she decides to dress up, too. After starting some soft music, I set the teakettle on to boil. Then I slice the fancy little cake I had bought at a bakery that afternoon and slide a piece onto Rachel's own fine china plate. I place a specially prepared gift bag next to her seat. Then I call for her to come.

Down the stairs she floats, humming along with the music. Slowly, curiously, she watches me. As she descends, I can tell she realizes what I wanted her to know at this moment: I only have eyes for her. She is the most special young heart in the entire world. The evening is devoted to her. And we are about to share a secret.

"Who is the present for?" she asks.

"You. But first, would you care for some tea and cake?"

"Why, yes. Thank you," she says, playing along.

I pour our tea, and in the gentle words I had rehearsed in my mind a dozen times, I tell her this is a special occasion. Soon her body will be changing. She will be leaving girlhood and entering the next amazing season of her life. I tell her this party is a celebration of those changes. As her mother, I want personally to welcome her to womanhood.

Her eyes open wide. Her heart is open even wider. And I am ready.

My explanations of the specific changes she can expect in her body are clear. I am not embarrassed. I speak with knowledge and authority but also with tender respect. I invite her to ask questions.

In a hushed voice she says, "Boys don't have anything like this happen to them every month, do they?"

"No," I tell her. "Only a woman's body is designed this way. Only a woman can carry and nurture new life. Men can't do that. Neither can angels. Only women."

We sit in silent wonder, sipping our tea and watching the pure white snowflakes as they swirl outside the front window.

"It's an honor to be a woman then, isn't it?" Rachel says.

That thought had never settled on me before. Slowly, I nod my agreement. "Yes, it is an honor. A great honor."

"You said this present was for me…." Rachel glances at the gift bag.

"Yes, you may open it now, if you'd like."

She pulls out the small bottle of kiwi-strawberry-scented body spray and grins. "You remembered. This is my favorite." The tiny gold box that holds the two coconut truffles also brings a smile to her face. She pauses when she uncovers the small, pink box of panty liners.

"I wondered when I was going to get some of these. This is the same kind Meredith has. I saw them in her closet once, and I thought maybe I would have to ask you to get me some." She looks up. "I'm glad I didn't have to ask."

I tell her that I want her always to feel free to ask me anything. Any time. She promises she will.

We pray together, and I listen as my daughter thanks God for making her body a woman's body. I realize that I have never thanked God for that. I have never thanked Him that everything about my body worked and that twice I was privileged to nurture and bear new life. I'm stunned by the miracle of it all and find myself praying deeply and fervently, as if this celebration were designed to give me a thankful heart.

With my eyes now opened in more ways than one, I smile at the living miracle sitting beside me. "How should we conclude our party?" I ask her.

"I think we should dance," Rachel says. This child danced before she walked. She hears a story in every refrain and has spent the first decade of her life translating every song she's ever heard into some form of dance. Of course our party should end with dancing. I realize that for almost an hour now, the music has been beckoning her to respond. And so she does. Free and innocent, honored and awed, full of life, Rachel responds.

Outside, the lacy snowflakes twirl in their enchanting dance of winter. In my heart I bask in the amber glow as the season of my own life changes from summer to fall. And there, before the cozy fire, I watch my only daughter as she blossoms in the fragrant fullness of springtime and waltzes, unashamed, into womanhood.

The time we spend teaching our daughters—

biological and spiritual—

about the joys and responsibilities of womanhood

will provide benefits for generations to come.

EMILIE BARNES

What a Mother Thinks

I love you so much.

There is no way

I can possibly put into words

how proud I am of you.

You're absolutely beautiful.

Sometimes when our eyes meet,

It's like gazing into a reflecting pool.

I see in you glimmers of my past.

Do you see in me hints of your future?

You are everything I ever prayed for.

There's nothing about you I'd change.

I love you more than you will ever know,

More than you will ever ask.

There's nothing I wouldn't give for you,

Nothing I wouldn't do for you.

You are my daughter,

And I will always love you

with a love so immense

so eternal

I could never find a way

to squeeze it into words.

RACHEL'S STORY

Last year I was in gym class when my friend Shannon came running up to me. "Rachel, come with me to the nurse's office."

We got a pass from our teacher, and on the way to the office, I asked her what was wrong. She kept crying. I stopped walking. "Tell me, Shannon! Are you sick?"

"No," she said. "I'm just scared."

"Why?"

She looked down and in a low voice said, "I'm bleeding. I think I just started my period."

I couldn't understand why she was so upset. "That's great! Congratulations! I'm happy for you."

She thought I was making fun of her.

"No," I told her, "I'm serious. I really am happy for you. You shouldn't be afraid. This is what your body is supposed to do. It's kind of a miracle."

Shannon calmed down, and we kept walking to the office. I didn't say anything else, but the whole way I was thinking, *Why isn't she excited about this? Didn't her mom have a special tea party for her and welcome her into womanhood?*

I asked her if she kind of understood what was happening inside her, and she said all she knew was what they taught us at school.

I felt sad for her. No girl should ever feel afraid or ashamed of what happens when her body changes. I think every girl who leaves the island of childhood for the mainland of adulthood should make that crossing on a party boat or be pampered on a luxury liner. No girl should be expected to swim there on her own!

When we reached the nurse's office, we had to wait. Eventually I went back to gym class by myself because the nurse was extra nice and said Shannon could stay there the rest of the class time.

After school that day, I fixed up a gift box for Shannon and took it over to her house. It had a few pampering-type gifts along with some feminine essentials. I told her it was my own little welcome-to-womanhood present. From one young woman to another. On the card I had written some of my favorite verses from Psalm 139. She loved the gift and told me her whole day had been terrible, but this was the one nice thing that had happened to her.

I've already thought about doing something special for my youngest cousin when she gets a little older. Every girl needs someone to remind her that she's special and to make the crossing over to womanhood a really wonderful celebration.

You made all the delicate,

inner parts of my body,

and knit them together

in my mother's womb.

Thank you for making me

so wonderfully complex!...

PSALM 139:13 [TLB]

Celebration Suggestions from My Friends

KATHLEEN: We had four girls in our family. When our youngest sister started to borrow personal-care stuff from the rest of us, we decided to give her something special for her birthday. We cleared one of the drawers in the bathroom and told her she could have that drawer for herself. Then we pooled our money and bought her a bagful of brand-new girl-stuff like lip gloss, nail polish and remover, tweezers, lotion, cotton balls, astringent, facial masque, body shampoo, scented foaming shaving cream, and a bag of disposable razors. The three of us older sisters promised her that for the next two months, we wouldn't borrow any of her new personal-care stuff.

She loved the goodies, and suddenly the three of us were "working" on her. Our bathroom turned into a beauty salon for the next three hours as we taught our fledgling how to pluck, file, condition, and exfoliate. She asked questions about the changes beginning to happen in her body. As the three of us offered advice, we realized that soon all four of us would be women. A unique bond grew that was never there before.

After that it became a tradition for the four of us to give each other a bagful of girl-stuff on our birthdays and to follow it up with what our dad called a "beauty session" in our bathroom.

I've been married for eight years, and my husband still doesn't understand why I get so thrilled when one of my sisters sends me a box of personal-care items for my birthday. I just wish my sisters were around to give me a facial!

CASSIE: Last spring our local hospital hosted an event in which several nurses gave a workshop on puberty. Another homeschool mom and I took our daughters to the event. Even though less than a dozen moms and daughters were there, our girls seemed too self-conscious even to eat the cookies and punch offered to them.

When we left the hospital, we spontaneously decided to have our nails done. We were having so much fun that we extended the afternoon into a long walk along the lake trail. Instead of the preteens pairing up for the walk, our daughters drew near to us moms. We paced ourselves as two mother-daughter couples so that we couldn't overhear each other's conversations.

The questions my daughter asked then were the ones that had gone unanswered at the hospital. "How does it feel inside when you start?" "How old were you, Mom?" "What happens at night when you're asleep?"

Toward the end of the trail, my daughter slipped her hand with her pretty painted nails in mine and said, "I'm glad you're walking with me through this. I don't think I could figure out all this on my own."

Our relationship changed that day. I felt a little sad that I'd never had a day like that with my mother. But I was thrilled for the openness I could now have with my daughter.

HANNAH: When my brother asked me to have a talk with his daughter about growing up, he suggested I take her to a nice restaurant or away for a weekend. I knew I would be more comfortable in the quietness of my own dining room. I mailed her a fancy invitation and set the table with all my finest. The plate she ate from was her own china plate, which her grandmother had given her two years before.

When she realized where the conversation was going, she told me she already knew the basics. I had practiced so diligently to explain everything just right that I felt deflated. She didn't need me.

But then our elegant party turned into something different than an information session. It became an afternoon of discussing the mystery of womanhood. Even though we were alone, our voices were hushed as we imagined aloud what God must have been thinking when he created man and woman. All we could find in my Bible was that God said it was "very good."

I think she left knowing that I highly esteemed her, and that the way her body was developing meant that God was doing something good in her life. At that age all girls need to be reminded that something very good is happening.

Items you need before passing on the mystery of womanhood:

- A time set aside for just the two of you

- A gift bag with a few personal girl-items, such as: panty liners; a small, zippered bag to keep pads organized, clean, and concealed in purse or backpack; body splash or powder; a small calendar

- A good reference book from a bookstore or library to help you feel comfortable with the specifics of puberty and reproduction as you give her information and answer questions

Other suggestions:

- If the opportunity allows, go away for a weekend, just the two of you, and do little things to help her feel grown-up.

- Invite other women with whom she is close to come to a special party in her honor. Ask the older women to share their wisdom with her.

- Go on a mother-daughter church retreat and set aside a special time for the two of you during the weekend.

THE DREAM OF SEVEN WILD

A Scandinavian folktale suggests a fanciful way for a young maiden to take a peek at her future true love. According to the tradition, if a young woman picks seven wildflowers on midsummer's eve and sleeps with them under her pillow, she will dream of the man she is going to marry.

I found this whimsical tradition intriguing. But then, I was raised on fairy tales, legends, and stories about Narnia.

As a child I turned a blue shoebox into a cottage for the flower fairies, which I felt certain lived in our garden. The cottage wasn't fancy. A simple spool served as their table. Two plastic thimbles were the chairs. A matchbox stuffed with cotton made a lovely bed. I remember coloring tiny pictures on the "walls" of the shoebox and gathering orphan buttons from my mother's sewing basket to use as dinner plates.

So when my daughter entered middle school and appropriately blushed on cue whenever my husband teased her about boys, I wanted to enter into the fanciful world that was opening up to her. I wondered if this might be a good time to make use of the Scandinavian folklore and take my young maiden into the woods on midsummer's eve in search of seven wildflowers.

Rachel's friend Karen was sleeping over that night. I knocked on Rachel's bedroom door at about three o'clock that afternoon and asked the girls if they would like to go for a walk. Of course, they said no. Then I told them about the folktale and asked again if they would be interested in picking some wildflowers.

The two friends exchanged glances. They both shrugged and said, "Okay, I guess."

However, their faces gave away their true feelings. Both of them sported rosy cheeks while tiny wish-glimmers danced in their eyes.

Off we went, three women to the woods on a mission.

"Do the flowers have to be different colors?" Karen asked.

I said I didn't think it mattered.

"What if both of us have the same flowers?" Rachel wanted to know. "Will we end up dreaming about the same guy?"

I said I didn't think so.

Karen plucked a droopy purple flower. "What if this one is actually a pretty weed and not a flower at all?"

I couldn't suppress my laughter another minute. "Ladies, this is only pretend! It's just for fun. It's whimsy. We can make it whatever we want it to be."

"We are making it what we want it to be," Rachel said.

I kept my lips sealed as their "supposing" and "what if-ing" continued. They seemed to enjoy the adventure more by having their own set of rules, one of which was that the flowers must be pressed.

As soon as we returned home, each of them clutching a fistful of wildflowers, they went to work pressing their bouquets. Karen carefully placed the flowers between two paper towels. Rachel found the largest dictionary in the house to put on top. Then they took turns sitting on the dictionary, coaxing the flowers to squish promptly.

Our afternoon conversation was sprinkled with glee. I loved being included in their discussion about guys and what they thought the future would bring. I knew the two of them had held these sorts of hushed discussions behind closed doors, but this was the first time they had invited me to join in. All because of my suggestion that we tromp through the woods to gather dreams about their future love lives.

"How did you know you loved Dad?" Rachel asked from her perch on the dictionary. "I mean, how did you know you were in love?"

I told them my love story, complete with all the frills. They soaked up the details, and I felt happy and mushy and very young again.

By bedtime, the flowers were flat. Beneath the girls' pillows the flowers went, arranged just so. Blue, yellow, white, and orange. I smiled at the agreeable little ambassadors from the land of sweet dreams. What wonderful conversation starters those flowers had turned out to be!

I tucked Rachel and Karen into bed. They giggled again about what their imaginations might show them during the night.

"I hope I can see his face when I dream," Karen said. "I hate it when I have a really good dream, but then I wake up and I can't remember who was in the dream."

"I know," Rachel agreed. "Or when you're in the middle of a dream, and the guy is just about to say something, and then you wake up. I get so mad when that happens."

"You said this afternoon that you prayed for your future husband," Karen said to me. "When do you think we should start praying about our future husbands?"

I smiled because I knew the answer. I just never expected them to ask the question.

Sitting on the edge of Rachel's bed, I stroked her hair and told her for the first time that I had been praying for her future husband since the day she was born.

"Your mom and I have talked about this," I told Karen. "I happen to know that your mom has been praying the same for you."

The girls were pleased. Neither seemed especially surprised. They settled in under their covers as a restful calm came over us.

"I think we should pray for our future husbands tonight," Karen said softly.

"I know. I was just thinking the same thing," Rachel said. "Do you want to pray with us, Mom?"

Of course I did. This was far more wonderful than I had hoped it would be. We joined hands and prayed. Solemn words tiptoed from these two young hearts and winged their way to the courts of heaven.

I placed my hand on Rachel and Karen's foreheads and blessed them. Turning out the light, I closed the door. I could hear them whispering. I thought of how their guardian angels must be hiding in the moonbeams of this delightful, midsummer's eve. And I could almost see the celestial beings winking at each other.

Daylight brought a gurgling brook of stories about the dream-filled night. Karen almost saw "his" face, but then he turned away. Rachel was certain the guy she saw in her dream had dark hair. That made her happy; she likes guys with dark hair. Karen's dream held only blonds.

The stories expanded over the breakfast table. The details grew. The men in the house shook their heads. They didn't understand. And we didn't expect them to. This was our own womanly whimsy. I watched as Rachel and Karen exchanged secret, subtle expressions, just like a couple of winking guardian angels.

DREAM-LOVE

Young Love lies sleeping
In May-time of the year,
Among the lilies,
…Young Love lies dreaming;
But who shall tell the dream?

CHRISTINA ROSSETTI

You have a very special place in my heart....
PHILIPPIANS 1:7 (TLB)

Dear Robin,

If you can believe this, I still have those wildflowers that Rachel and I picked on midsummer's eve when I was eleven. Even at almost sixteen, those flowers are symbolic for me.

I've put each of the flowers, like a bookmark, in my Bible by verses that are special to me. I guess you could say that the verses are promises from God, and the flowers remind me to stay true to my promise to trust God with the future.

The yellow flower is in Jeremiah 29. I underlined verse 11, "'For I know the plans I have for you,' says the LORD 'They are plans for good and not for evil, to give you a future and a hope'" (TLB). I love that promise!

The reddish flower is at the first chapter of Song of Solomon and sort of represents the whole book. I put it there because once I was thinking about how great it would be to share my whole life and everything with one man. And then I thought, Why would I want to ruin any of that future intimacy by giving away anything too soon to the wrong person? The wildflower reminds me to stop and wait for God's best.

Psalm 13 is where I put the blue flower. If you read that chapter, it might seem kind of strange because it starts off saying "How long will you forget me, Lord?" But it ends saying "I will always trust in you and in Your steadfast love" (TLB). That's the part I underlined. I want to remember that God has His very best already planned for me. I know that I can trust Him.

I've told a lot of my friends about the wildflowers and why I have them pressed in my Bible. I know God takes promises very seriously. And so do I. I don't know if I would have felt this way if we had never gone into the woods that one midsummer's eve. It's funny to think that a handful of pressed flowers could have meant so much not only during my teenage years but also for my whole future. And yet they have.

In Him,
Karen

I was asleep
but my heart was awake.

SONG OF SONGS 5:2 [NASB]

Dear God

RUTH BELL GRAHAM [AGE 19]

Dear God, I prayed, all unafraid

(as we're inclined to do)

I do not need a handsome man

But let him be like You;

I do not need one big and strong

nor yet so very tall,

Nor need he be some genius

Or wealthy, Lord, at all;

But let his head be high, dear God,

And let his eye be clear,

His shoulders straight, whate'er his state,

Whate'er his earthly sphere;

And let his face have character,

A ruggedness of soul,

And let his whole life show, dear God,

A singleness of goal;

Then when he comes (as he will come)

with quiet eyes aglow,

I'll understand that he's the man

I prayed for long ago.

Ruth married Billy Graham on August 13, 1943.

Celebration Suggestions from My Friends

MAUREEN: Years ago when my mother was in Sweden, she picked some wildflowers and made a prayer-wish for her future husband. She dried the flowers and kept them in a box. Her grandmother gave her a special handkerchief to use on her wedding day; so my mother sewed the pressed flowers into the folded handkerchief and then sewed the flattened handkerchief into the bodice of her wedding gown, next to her heart. No one knew they were there except my mother. She removed the handkerchief after the wedding, opened it, and added a pressed rosebud from her wedding bouquet.

The handkerchief remained tucked in her dresser drawer for years. I found it one day, and she told me the secret of those hidden, dried flowers. I think I'm the only one who knows that that lumpy, folded bit of cotton holds a world of dreams come true for her.

ANGELA: When our daughter, Taletha, was born, my husband was overseas. He wrote a tender letter to her, and I kept it in a box with her baby clothes. Taletha loves to paint. A few years ago she painted flowers around the edge of a picture frame and said she was going to save it until she had a picture of her boyfriend to put in it and hang on the wall.

The next summer we did our mother-daughter bonding thing by picking the wildflowers and talking about her future husband. When she went to bed that night and was all ready to put her flowers under her pillow, I told her I had a present for her. In the frame Taletha had painted, I had put the letter from her daddy. She had never read it before, and she burst into tears. I told her she should always remember there was a man in her life who loved her before she was born.

A few days later my husband said to me, "I don't know what you women did at your flower party the other night, but Taletha has been treating me like a prince ever since."

KRISTI: Last summer I took all the girls in our youth group on an overnight camping trip. It wasn't midsummer's eve, but we made up our own Dream Party. Each girl picked one wildflower to put under her pillow. When we sat around the campfire, we took turns saying what quality we looked for in guys. I read 1 Corinthians 13, the love chapter, to them by firelight, and then we talked about what qualities we should each start working on in our own lives.

The best part was the next morning. It was raining. We all huddled in the biggest tent, passing around a box of little powdered sugar donuts and telling about our wildflower dreams. We laughed so hard!

The next week one girl told me that when she heard all the other girls talking about their high standards she realized she needed to think more highly of herself. She told me she had stopped chasing this one guy she liked and had decided to "hold out for a hero" because she knew God wanted only the best for her.

That was the best thing that could have ever happened to this girl. Her older sister got pregnant at sixteen, and I was afraid she was following down the same path. That one night with the wildflowers may have changed her whole life.

In preparation for the dream of seven wildflowers:

- If you don't live near a place where wildflowers grow, plan ahead and plant in pots a variety of wildflowers that will be in bloom on midsummer's eve or pluck flowers on vines such as honeysuckle. Go to a flower shop and buy seven colorful flowers.

- Use two sheets of dainty stationery to press the flowers between heavy books.

- Give your special, young-hearted woman a diary to journal her private thoughts and feelings.

- Write out your love story and give it to her if you think she would appreciate having it when she's older.

Other suggestions:

- Plan an outing, camping trip, or even a backyard sleep-out. Make it a yearly tradition during which you retell your love story and talk about how your young companion has grown or changed since last year.

- Have the pressed flowers laminated and made into bookmarks.

Gentle Passages
Guiding Your Daughter into Womanhood

Published by Multnomah Gifts, a division of Multnomah® Publishers, Inc.
© 2002 by Robin Jones Gunn

Vist Robin's Web site at www.robingunn.com

ISBN 1-57673-943-0

Published in association with the literary agency of Janet Kobobel Grant,
Books & Such, 4788 Carissa Ave., Santa Rosa, CA 95405

Designed by Koechel Peterson & Associates, Minneapolis, Minnesota

Scripture quotations are taken from The Holy Bible, *New International Version*
© 1973, 1984 by International Bible Society, used by permission of Zondervan
Publishing House; *The Living Bible* (TLB) © 1971 by Tyndale House Publishers;
and *New American Standard Bible*® (NASB)
© 1960, 1977, 1995 by the Lockman Foundation; The Holy Bible,
New King James Version (NKJV) 1984 by Thomas Nelson, Inc.

Poem by Ruth Bell Graham taken from *Collected Poems*,
Baker Books, © 1997, 1992, 1997, 1998.
Used by permission.

Multnomah is a trademark of Multnomah
Publishers, Inc., and is registered in the U.S.
Patent and Trademark Office. The colophon
is a trademark of Multnomah Publishers, Inc.

For information:
   Multnomah Publishers, Inc.
   P.O. Box 1720
   Sisters, OR 97759

Printed in China

05 06 07 — 10 9 8 7 6 5 4 3

www.multnomahgifts.com